Things I Like

I Like Outer Space

Angela Aylmore

H **www.heinemann.co.uk/library**
Visit our website to find out more information about Heinemann Library books.

To order:
☎ Phone 44 (0) 1865 888066
Send a fax to 44 (0) 1865 314091
📄 Visit the Heinemann Bookshop at www.heinemann.co.uk/library to browse our
💻 catalogue and order online.

First published in Great Britain by Heinemann Library,
Halley Court, Jordan Hill, Oxford OX2 8EJ, part
of Harcourt Education. Heinemann is a registered
trademark of Harcourt Education Ltd.

Editorial: Dan Nunn and Sarah Chappelow
Design: Joanna Hinton-Malivoire
Picture research: Erica Newbery
Production: Duncan Gilbert

Origination: Chroma Graphics (Overseas) Pte. Ltd
Printed and bound in China by South
China Printing Co. Ltd.

10-digit ISBN 0 431 10954 0
13-digit ISBN 978 0 431 10954 1
11 10 09 08 07
10 9 8 7 6 5 4 3 2 1

British Library Cataloguing in Publication Data
Aylmore, Angela
I like outer space. - (Things I like)
1. Outer space - Juvenile literature
I. Title
520
A full catalogue record for this book is available from
the British Library.

Acknowledgements
The publishers would like to thank the following for
permission to reproduce photographs: Corbis pp. **6**
(Royalty-Free), **8** (Bill Ross), **14–15** (Roger Ressmeyer),
17 (NASA), **18**, **21** (Roger Ressmeyer), **22** (rocket, Roger
Ressmeyer); Getty Images/Photodisc pp. **4–5** (all), **13**,
22 (Saturn and telescope); Science Photo Library pp. **7**
(Frank Zullo), **10–11**; Science Photo Library/NASA pp. **9**,
12, **16** (both), **19**, **20**.

Cover photograph of an astronaut reproduced with
permission of Science Photo Library.

Every effort has been made to contact copyright holders
of any material reproduced in this book. Any omissions
will be rectified in subsequent printings if notice is given
to the publishers.

Contents

Some words are shown in bold, **like this**. You can find out what they mean by looking in the Glossary.

Outer space

I like outer space.

I will tell you my favourite things about it.

My telescope

I like to look at the stars.

I use my **telescope** to help me see them.

With my telescope,
I can see the Moon.

The dark holes are
called **craters**.

Planets

There are lots of planets in space. These are the planets that are closest to Earth.

Neptune

Uranus

Saturn

Jupiter

Mars

Earth

Venus

Mercury

11

This is Jupiter. It has a big red spot that looks like an eye.

My favourite planet is Saturn.
It has rings made from dust
and rock.

rings

Into space

I would like to go up into space. I would travel in a rocket.

I would live on a
space station.

The Earth would be a
very long way away.

I would wear a spacesuit.

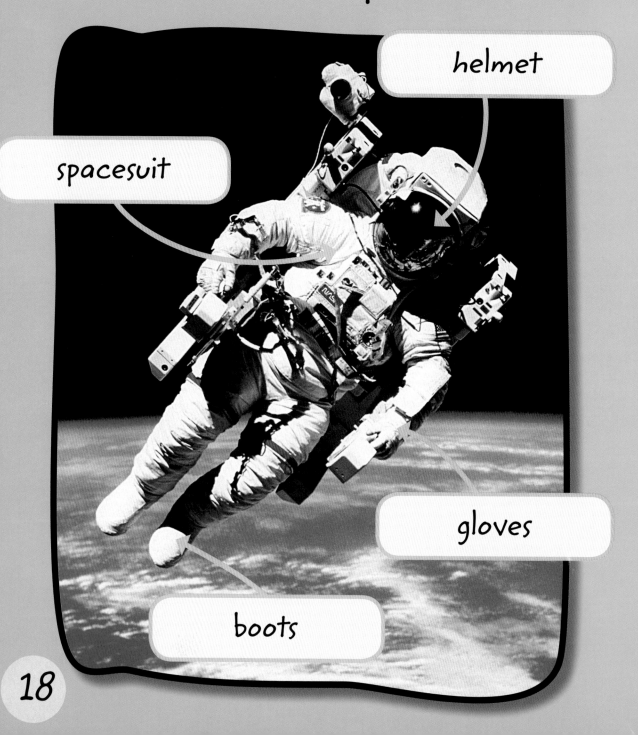

helmet

spacesuit

gloves

boots

jet pack

I would have a **jet pack** that would help me on my **missions**.

The best bit would be
walking on the Moon.

I would bring home a
moon rock to keep.

Do you like outer space?

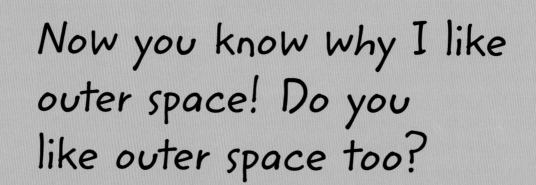

Now you know why I like outer space! Do you like outer space too?

Glossary

crater a large hole in the ground

jet pack special backpack used to move around in space

mission a special job that needs doing

rocket type of spaceship, used to blast into space

space station a large spaceship that stays in space all the time

telescope something used to make far away objects look bigger

Find out more

Check out this NASA website for kids:

www.nasa.gov/audience/forkids/kidsclub/flash/index.html

Take a tour of the universe and play some space games on this website:

www.windows.ucar.edu/

Index

24